The Good and The Evil

The Good and The Evil

COOPER HARRISON

RESOURCE *Publications* · Eugene, Oregon

THE GOOD AND THE EVIL

Resource Publications
An Imprint of Wipf and Stock Publishers
199 W. 8th Ave., Suite 3
Eugene, OR 97401

www.wipfandstock.com

PAPERBACK ISBN: 978-1-7252-8913-0
HARDCOVER ISBN: 978-1-7252-8914-7
EBOOK ISBN: 978-1-7252-8915-4

12/21/20

I dedicate this to those that suffer from a mental illness, the shackles of depression and vice. To the ones who feel controlled by society, I hope you can find peace and comfort with this work.

Contents

Acknowledgments

I would like to thank my teachers, my editor, my friends, and my family most importantly. Without them, I would not have written the poetry that I have written to this day. I would not have had the courage to publish not one, but two poetry books. Here's to many more books to come after this one.

Introduction

The purpose of this book is to build off *Virtues & Vices*. The first book is supposed to teach us what life can bring us that is good and what is evil. The cardinal virtues and deadly sins are in our everyday life. This book discusses our everyday temptations along with the good life has to offer. We have to learn to balance some things in life as well.

As you embark on this rigorous journey for the next 100 pages or so, challenge yourself to find out your evils that you must face. I did not say avoid, I said face. Facing our fears is like facing our demons. . . In order to conquer them, we must challenge them head-on and win. This also takes adversity and courage. Do you have courage? Or do you have to be afraid?

My last piece is that most (not all) of these poems are about my life events. From cancer to being bullied and abused by toxic relationships with a significant other. If you relate, I want you to know that you are a strong man, woman, or just even a person no matter the gender. I am proud of you and I hope you get something good out of this read. I love you, enjoy.

PART I

The Good

The Good is what we yearn for. . . The innate nature of it lies within our mind, our heart, and our soul. What makes us different from the apes is our ability to be good to each other. Our ability to help one another succeed and to show love. The good is innocent, it is pure, it is joyous, and it is bliss. . .

I am a lost soul.
Trying to be found.
Take me home.
Safe and sound.

—*My Keeper*

The light woke me up from my slumber on a cool Saturday morning. I had a long Friday night, but that is over now. It is Saturday and it is a new day and I am still on this Earth for a reason. A reason that cannot be explained, but a powerful reason at that. So I am going to attack this day with passion and excellence.

.

It's such a gift to us
from the time we wake
to the time we fuss

we can do what we want every single day
that is the beauty of the life we live
never letting good times ever go away

love who you are, love what you do
without seeing the good in each day
happiness is something you cannot accrue

each day has something special to offer
you always can "learn something new"
an opportunity to make our world alter

never look at the events in the past
because there's no time like livin' in the now
so stop making yourself feel like you're in last

with a new day comes time to improve
greater our strengths, build on our faults
then when we reach the end we will approve

take each and every day to make life count
we only have so many given to us
and always know we have such a great amount

—*The Days are Gifts*

it was all a dream to my perception
but in truth it was all a reality
something my mind thought was deception

dreams are good, but only happen in your sleep
you wake up and then they cease to exist
can even lead you to a place to weep

my teachers said I could not achieve anything, no sir
i did not amount to much in the classroom
but it gave me a bigger pot to stir

i was told I would never play a college sport
hurt me to the bottom of my heart
so I decided to go ahead and send a retort

people have always doubted me from the beginning
now I have temptations all around me
where the snakes lurk to watch me sinning

the focus is to one day have flashing lights
not from cop sirens, but from cameras
after I conquer all of life's fights

somebody I hope to make our world better
hose are the visions I have every night
let the poems I write be the world's letters

—it was all a dream

z
z z
z z
z z z z z z z

I love people. . .   all people
Keep the mind unlocked, it is the only way to grow
              Without growth there is no prosperity
                          Worldly objects can come and go
                          But friendships last an eternity
              Don't just tolerate, but accept
              Accept all walks of life
              Listen to the struggles of others
Lord knows we all have it. . .   So dig for your identity
       Show your growth not to just your friends or family
              But to those you even dislike
Hear the other story and embrace them. Be open to growth. . .

                    —open to acceptance

Respecting myself for my own sake.
Been walked on like your bathroom floor and it is needing a deep clean. . .
I just hope you understand why.
That there are walls that my heart created for a reason and that my body will abide by.
I still hurt from the past that needs time to heal and resolve.
I promise you though. . .
I. . .
Am. . .
Worth. . .
The. . .
Wait. . .

—Prudence

You came to me.
Trusted me with your body,
your mind,
your soul.
We made magic, but love stemmed from this.
Not lust,
Not selfish desires,
but love.
You satisfied my wants and needs.
While I hoped to satisfy yours.
Love me like you do,
and let me do the same.
Let me fill you up with love.
I won't use your body for pleasure.
I will use your heart,
but give you mine in the process.
Fill my spirit as I fill yours tonight.

—*Sex with Love*

We rely on so many people in order to survive and become great. It is that love from someone that is so unceasing. What would we do without it? Would we crumble? Would we fall? This love is unceasing, but we seem to take it for granted. It's a privilege that not everyone still has. It's more used when it's "convenient." They still will never let that love die. We should be grateful. We should love like they love us too.

—*A Parent's Love*

It grows in a dry and desolate place,
But it still grows in beauty and awe
It doesn't need water and nourishment
It needs admiration and endearment
But the dangers lurk in the desert
The wild beasts want to stalk her
So she protects herself with sharp thorns
Making it difficult to approach her
For worry of the pain she must exacerbate
Her looks are appetizing, but she's prudent
She knows better than that
Her roots are her stronghold,
But they lie below the surface
You can't see how beautiful her heart can show
Because degenerates only value her exterior
She's the only rose in the desert
Waiting. . . waiting to be picked
Not just by anyone
But someone who is gentle
Someone who is loving
Someone who is caring
The rose will choose who picks her
She will let her thorns diminish
And embrace her new home
Filled with happiness, laughter, and love
Where she will never wilt
Never wade
Never decease
Fight on, desert flower
You will be picked soon enough
And brighten one's life
Brighten one's household
Brighten one's future
Soon, sweet desert rose
Soon oh so soon

—A Desert Rose

it can hurt more than anything
even if it seems too good to be
sometimes it can be a sign, like a wedding ring

the truth is not always so depressing
we have made the word so cad
when cruel people tend to keep misconstruing

they always say "The truth will set you free"
we must stay honest to that
instead of manipulating and preventing people from who they should be

the idea of it is supposed to hurt
growing thick skin is actually important at times
you can't sugar coat to just be curt

our politicians may lack this trait
but not all hope is lost
our world truth is coming, just you wait.

— *Truth*

It's the last thing we think about. . .   Why?
It should be the first thing we do when we wake
The world gets loud sometimes,
        Even scary as hell to us.
The most forgetful part of life
And the least consistent too,
        We seem to not find the time.
When's it's clearly there for us to use.

—Self-care

Nobody can replicate this being.
The power is incomparable.
If knowledge is power then this surpasses all.
Most of the world believes in it,
but this can turn the critics into believers.
The love and mercy conquers all evil.
So we all can enter the kingdom.
Or maybe enter the next life
Spending eternal life filled with happiness.
A happiness greater than our understanding

—A Higher Power

You'll lose yourself without it
Find gratification in the wrong places
With love coming from the wrong people
Then you're hated when you are "found"
People do not want you happy with yourself
The leeches of society want you sad
They thrive on misery, anger, and stress
And when you are gone, you are forgotten

Well. . . don't need your approval of me then!
I don't need the sex, the drugs, the social accreditation

All I need is validation from myself
My family and the ones I love most
    The people who won't abandon me if I fail,
   or won't judge me for going in a different direction.
    For I stand upon the beauty of my heart
     and soul not just my smile or my talk
You go ahead and sell your soul though
I will go enjoy the life I want to live
A life of Love, Freedom, and Devotion to good
To my higher calling
My family
My friends
My inner being

  —Authenticity

"Amazing Grace, how sweet"... she sounds
her feelings seem real in my eyes
why should I trust her? What has she proven to me?
She's been with plenty of men, far greater than I.
Is she worth the heartache? The stress? The tears?
Yes, I give her the consent to break my heart.
The pain in the end will be paid in full...
By the joy she has given me before all the hurt.
She's the one where I stop thinking...
Thinking about my exes and saying "what if."
This girl will crash into me like a wave,
A wave of happiness that'll crush the hate and the despair.
What makes us great is that we have the greatest virtue of all.
It may conquer,
but we must choose it first.
If we do not then our world is lost.

It is that warm feeling you get with that special someone.
That someone that makes you forget all your insecurities
All of your imperfections.
They just want to show you...
That you are valued,
that you are cherished,
that you are the best.
To them,
Even when nobody else felt the same.
They will help you grow,
but pick you up when you fall.
To help you succeed,
no matter how big the dream may be.
Bring you closer to maturity,
but still make sure you enjoy life's moments.
All with innocence and...

    —True Love

There when you need
There when you call
There when you succeed
There when you fail
There for your ups
There for your downs
There for your smiles
There for your frowns
There to hype you up
There to tone you down
There to reward you
There to scold you
No matter what though, they are always there for you.

—Real Friends

If only we used these more. . .
Instead of making people our emotional punching bags, we could utilize a
qualified person.

—*A Therapist*

The late night calls. The struggles they sometimes add to your life.

They won't even doubt you. They won't even leave your side.

They want your suffering. They want all of
your pain.

—*That One Friend*

There ain't no perfect, but paint a perfect picture.

But it's with your loved ones and they are with you.

If you ain't walking with it, you walk by sight.

Chin up since things won't go your way.

Ideally life calls for hardship and pressure.

We make mistakes, but every time it is new.

Let go of hate and stop your fight.

Get off Twitter cause only your loved ones care what you say.

—Faith

your heart might be in the right place
but only your mind can tell you what's right and what's wrong

—*Conscience*

it's like sunshine and rainbows
when they tell you sweet somethings
hold you and never let go
you'll never want to leave
or for the day to end. . .

      —A Significant Other

Go back to your night clubs
worry about being popular
I'm just trying to collect pay stubs.

Holding me back from deserved greatness
separate yourself though
don't let talent be affected by the fakeness.

The time to yourself is time you never forget
the moments you grow
and the moments that won't end in regret.

Working hard to create memories
be methodical with your time
instead of using all the remedies.

If tempted with a good time
take a step back to discover the internal
don't go out and be other people's mime.

Find your priority
but choose wisely
to be a wealthy minority.

—*Sacrifices*

You found me battered and broken
You picked me up though
and put all the pieces back together
to watch me grow. . .

It's amazing. . .
Watching yourself grow from your mistakes. Growing from your faults and shortcomings. Overcoming the odds to become the best version of yourself. Learning from each and every heartbreak that somehow still has so much meaning. Finding purpose in things we thought never deserved our time and attention. Perfecting our craft and critiquing our every move that we make. Realizing that our weaknesses can become our strengths if we just work it and don't become complacent. Changing the things that we are tired of noticing. Not just so other people can love us, but that we start to love ourselves. So when we do fall we can pick ourselves up and become better. We only have one life, so let's make ourselves the best and brightest version. What a life we live.

—*Maturity*

                                        Where did the time go. . .
                        Seemed like yesterday
That I was just doing the same routine
With the same people
                                              In the same place

Like I am stuck

say this, say that, say whatever
but do this, do that, do better
the pen may be mightier than the sword
but in a fight, who you leaning toward?
the guarantees are nice to have and hear
but if they don't come to fruition you are a bier
words mean nothing
actions mean something

—Actions Speak Louder

"How are you today?"

Those four simple words can change someone's day.

I mean, you never know how someone feels.
Someone could be going through
A breakup or fight
A death in the family
They just got fired from their dream job
They failed a class

With not a single person to talk to about it.

I want to show you how I do it.
To support you and reinforce you.
Even when I do poorly, I still hope you succeed to help our team.
Hopefully you can look at me
and see a role model to guide you in a confusing world.
Teaching you to be a light to this darkness.
That is my plan. . .
So listen up, eyes here.
Watch me and learn.
And if I ever lead you astray. . .
Correct me and lead me.
Because we can learn from each other.
None of us are perfect. We should still strive for it
and show the younger generation
that we can be better

—*Lead By Example*

I waited for you all my life
this moment has been a dream
like a fairy tale
you just hope that it happens
even when you're single in college think you'll be alone forever.

thinking about how trash your desired gender is, when it's not the case.

then. . . boom, you see that person
they look so incredible. . .
you tense up and get nervous
worrying that you'll blow it.
"they'll think I'm weird" or
"it's just not the right time"
but you're just scared
to take that risk
even when it might hurt you
you still make that move
send that text
go on that date
give that kiss
meet those parents
get on that knee
recite those vows
and say "I do."
you go on that honeymoon
pursue those dreams
create some beautiful children
go through failures
lose loved ones in the process
contemplate friendships and other relationships
fight with one another
make fun of each other
get frustrated with the bond
second guess maybe. . .
but that is okay!
it's not going to be perfect
it's not going to be easy
there will be some struggles
it will make it stronger
because your other help should be there for you and your downfalls.

the beauty is in the struggle
pain brings ya'll closer
complacency pushes you away
tragedy strengthens the link
it's more than just "winning" because you win every single day.

coming home to your loving significant other and the little parts of you.

those people love you forever
don't ever turn your back on that
never lose sight of the great thing you worried about never having as a
lonely kid in college.

    —Marriage

People want to believe in good, but you have to give them a reason for it.

—*Trusting You*

It's a marathon, not a sprint.
Perfection takes time in life
It takes actual:

- Blood

- Sweat

- Tears

Change is not an overnight event.
It's not a song, but a symphony.

—Finding Yourself

I'll make my mistakes
Nobody is perfect
but I'm going to learn from them
and became a better version of myself

—Self-Awareness

It's a Sunday, it's okay to be lazy. . .

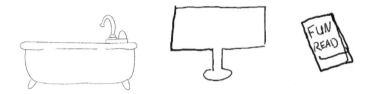

Take some time. . .
Have some coffee.
Throw on some Netflix or read a book.
Get a workout done or do some yoga.
Take a long, hot shower or bath.
Do a meditative exercise.
Sleep. . . Lord knows we all need that.

Don't be afraid to go to do soulful either.

We treated her like a can
Throwing our trash in her
Killing her beautiful children
In the sea,
In the air,
In the ground too
Without any regard for her well being
She will rain down consequences
Shake our world beneath us
Freeze over our happiness
While scorching our food supply
Unless we wake up
And start to make a change
Clean up our mistakes
Before it's too late!

—*Mother Nature*

Build my mind
Unleash my anger
Relinquish my stress
Clear my mind
Bury my sorrow
Embrace my grind
Fix my failure
Achieve my goals
Silence my critics
Conquer my opponents
Fuel my motivation
Feed my drive
Love my process

—Exercise

I kept it because I dislike fighting
sometimes it's best to let it go instead of making it bigger than what it is
setting aside our differences and finding our common ground
that is what we need to do in order for us to thrive as one
don't measure how big the gun is, measure how big your heart is
violence can conquer countries, but kindness remains king
so stop the shootings, bombings, and missile testing
start the conversation.

—*Peace*

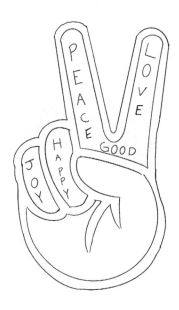

See the good in all things.
Fear no evil.

Do not just speak good.
Do the good.

You can become the light of the world.
You can become something great.

Life is like a movie.
Life can be a horror film or a comedy.

We have only one life.
So make that life count.

Good. . . Something we should strive to be in all days and in all things.

Each decision we make could be a lasting one.

Not everyone can make their own decisions.

Some people have no freedoms, no rights, nothing.

We face challenges all day, but the goodness given to us can prevail.

We just have to choose to use it.

PART II

The Evil

It lurks in the shadows, waiting to consume you whole. The evil is what casts a dark cloud over the beautiful world that we reside in. It takes on many forms and many shapes. It is not just demonic, but everyday life as well. It is the little things and little habits that can corrupt the mind. What evils are lingering over your conscience?

you're never going to solve all your problems. . .
not in one night
so child of mine get some rest
you'll need it to be your best. . .

  —*Stress*

they come out at night when I am alone and afraid
to be someone I'm not, to put on a masquerade

they want me to harm myself
when in reality it just harms others like a coffin on the shelf

they need to leave before I implode
and hurt the ones when I unload

they prey on my insecurities
make me hate my impurities

they will conquer my soul
lord, please take this toll

—*Demons in My Head*

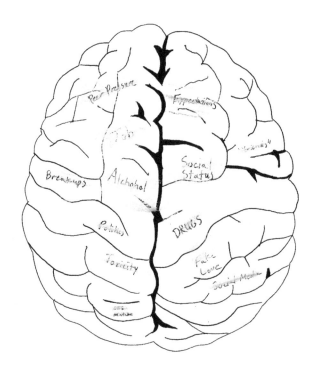

I bury haters like dead bodies
The ones who act nice to my face
Those females that want a real man but catch bodies

I write to those that hurt me well
The hurt that hits my mind, body, and soul
It angers me so much I want to just scream and yell

I put my heart and soul into all things
Sports, school, friends, and especially relationships
The girls that didn't treat me like one of the kings

I can list every time someone talked noise
Funny thing is it's always behind my back
Next time say it to my face before I lose poise

I'm a nice guy I really am once you know
But even nice guys can turn mean
Especially when this guy has a platform to show

I'll close this drama with a parting gift
Before you decide to hurt me or hate on me
Just know. . . I hurt and I sometimes don't uplift

—Bury The Hatchet With Vengeance

45

love the way it touches my lips
feels better than the kiss of a loved one
impair my judgement, my worries
especially with that only class I am failing
excuses are made when a "mistake" occurs
or I say something that I do not mean
blaming it on the alcohol is the best scapegoat
the brain tells me to stay in and read
the heart tells me to grab a bottle and chug
blacking out is my way to cope with life
even if my family tells me otherwise
just let me lower my standards for the night
and regret it all the next morning
the pain in my heart. . .
needs to be numbed. . .
let me drink. . .
the pain. . .
away. . .

—*My Drinking*

My heart hurts during this time
No girl to love me, make me feel special.
Sitting here just trying to rhyme
While everybody is out, high off being fallacial.

Loneliness they say is "good for the soul"
But what about the dark days?
I seem to lose myself down this dark hole
Until I hear what the higher power says. . .

"You know, I love you so much.
So do your friends and family,
You don't even need a woman's physical touch.
So stop acting with so much hammily."

There's no love on people's conscience
They won't come where I reside
People hate my success and are self-conscious
There's nobody I have to confide

The real ones are so few
I have to drop the manipulatives
And start my circle brand new
And add those that are commemorative

My circle is small, but I feel appreciated
It's about powerful conversation
And not getting inebriated
Because it's really about personal relation

—*Loneliness*

Who was there for me when best my friend died?
Who was there for me when I just cried?

Nobody's there for me when I'm in need,
Just go to church and say your creed.

Life goes on. . . People don't care
Their drama traps me. . . Just like a snare.

I have to block the ones who doubt
Cut off the negative energy, even the godforsaken "clout."

My real ones were there when cancer made me sick
They never came around just for a trick.

Ask me to run what I said back for clarity
With the assumption you'll get my sincerity.

I clean up everyone's mess,
With no one here for my stress.

When you lose your virginity at an age not so keen
                                    The views are just never the same
                We have education, but no morals for a teen

This good can become evil for many.
                                    It can corrupt our minds;
                The name of the game is to conquer plenty.

Why must we make this a weapon?
                                    It doesn't make any sense;
                To make something so pure, so treason.

It's so addicting and hard to break.
                                    Most humans do anything to obtain it,
                To the point where we sleep but never wake.

You'll lose friendships over this gift.
                                    It's with a higher purpose.
                Without it, creation will cease to exist.

Choose to use this wisely.
                                    If you do not,
                Deal with the consequences decisively.

—Sex Without Love

It's the pre-meditated murder:
of your relationship
of your significant other's mental health
of your friendships
of your own self-image
of your loved one's trust, forever
of your own lineage
of your reputation
of your mind
of your situation

—*Cheating*

most believe that they are deity
when most don't even act like they're human

the rich may rule the world
but nobody rules the universe

our weakest people look the strongest
while those with true strength still thrive

people tend to fly too high on life
resulting in deception and failing like Icarus

asking for help is for the weak they say
in reality, guidance is what we truly need

the labyrinth of life follies us time and time again
it can swallow us in the belly of the beast

walk tall and do not fall
fall on your own ego that is

your life is not more precious than the next
so don't try and demean your brother or sister

easy is where the expectation sets itself
difficult is the reality of life

go and thank those who gave you life
don't take it until it's taken from you

                —*Hubris*

Do not let the truth interfere with a good story. . .

Wait. . .

Yeah you actually should, because that's just lying. . .

I just want to take away my pain
Even though I might die in vain
My life is worth for those who slain

Maybe I'll just join the game
And kill my customers without shame
Feel no guilt because it's not my name

Let me get fucked up with my friends
The constant phrase that never ends
But they don't care, it's just for pretends

It could be the reason success hinders
Until our mind and independence turners to cinders
The addiction and want still lingers

We can cure cancer with some
Or kill others mostly from our scum
All just for a feeling that's numb

Just give me the needle, bring me low
I want a line, an upper, some blow
Pass me the blunt and let's take life slow

—*Drugs and Abuse*

he only left because she didn't do enough
playing the victim card like your name is OJ
but this crime fits you like a glove this time. . .

so who is right?
who is wrong?
who was the abuser though?
      who was the one who didn't let the other go out?
who reprimanded who behind closed doors?
who was the perpetrator?

      —Manipulation

When I'm alone
Those thoughts seep
They're of loneliness
Ones too deep

What scares most
Is the depression
Not just the fear
My own aggression

Nothing to say
Nothing to do
Can't be vocal
Only be true

Look at myself
Life in reflection
Can I see
My own selection

Right my wrongs
Myself to blame
Must be done
With no shame

—Lost and Abandoned

Breathe now. . .

do it for yourself and for your mental health
depression will come up in moments of stealth

breathe in the good and breathe out the hate
the evil that hinders you from being great

inhale the calm
exhale the qualm

ingest what God has provided, the positivity
excrete what Satan has provided, the negativity

let the air invigorate the soul
before the toxicity winds up taking control

the breath of life needs to be known
it came from birth in order to be grown

take away the breath, you take away life
something that cannot be forgiven by strife

Just breathe for me. . .

One of the greatest evils of all time
It killed so many great people, all from its intoxication
The one object that can lead anyone to Greed
Not even that, but Lust and Anger occur
Occur from the most pure at heart human.
This tangible object means vast amounts of power
This is a necessity to all people
We use this to run the world
And the decisions even made are affected by commerce
When it all runs out, what do you have?
Some have nothing though
Even when they have everything. . .
It can only buy happiness for so long
Call it the crutch of depression's relief
Only those who love are loved. . . can walk freely on a paved road
We chase and follow like helpless sheep
To the one thing that'll always be elusive
It cannot ever grow enough
To the point where you stop
It is the never ending cycle
Man made it, but Jesus resisted. . .
So does that make us Satan?
Does that make all of us "in the wrong"?
Not if it's shared, like ours
Saint Matthew and his 16 verse from his 25th chapter
Give yourself to others. . .

  —Money

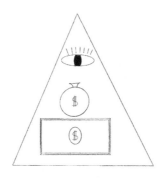

every death done too soon
it hurts my soul
no matter how much I knew
they're like my brother
my sister
my favorite human being
a family member of God
if only they had more memories to give
do not fret though
the lasting effect of each human will last
we will never forget
the great lives of our fallen

I am not perfect
I will never be perfect
My life is not perfect
My life will never be perfect
But that's alright
I will make myself better
I will make my life better
I will succeed
I will fail
I won't falter
And I will not expect perfection

—*Expectations vs. Reality*

$$\frac{\text{Perfection}}{\text{Reality}}$$

we judge those by their tone
not the tone of their voice, but their skin
these actions, our life does not condone
more worried about visual patriotism
we wear our colors proudly
except shootings, confederate flags, and political parties are our euphemisms
violence is our way we settle disputes
not just with our guns or knives
but even ruining lives with our suits
in the end, we all are not so different
               we all have a story
so stop showing anger that is so fervent
I am tired of people calling African Americans "thugs" or using the n word
to intimidate
I am sick of bigots stereotyping Muslims in airports and calling Hispanics
illegals
let's just love each other and love our cultures because are we not "the melt-
ing pot"?
is America not supposed to be the country that brings ALL people together?
sure doesn't look like it. . .

—*Racism*

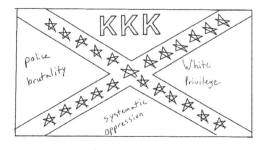

The few. . . the far. . . the in-between
The few that get the help they need
The far are the ones who get clean
The in-between are those who lack the guidance

—Addiction

I actually have. . . No, for real. This is true, I'm not making this up. No crutch is being used to justify for whenever I fail or misconceive someone.
I am not using this for clout.
I am not using this for free meds.
My issues are authentic and valid. My life consists of bullying, suicide, grudges, and inhumane punishment.
I want to be like everyone else.
But I can't be like everyone else.
Because I'm ill.
No, it's not the flu ill.
Physically, I feel fantastic.
Emotionally, I am an absolute wreck.
My spirituality is crushed.
My mental health. . . has deteriorated.

—*Depression*

A woman can do the equivalent
To what a man can do. . .

She can say as much as he can.
She can love, more than he can.
She can write, just as well as he can.
She can play, better than he can.
She can yell, louder than he can.
She can run, faster than he can.
She is learning, more than he can.
She is working, harder than he can.
But. . .

He is winning, more than she is.
He is paid, higher than she is.
He is treated, better than she is.

—Sexism

Drop the toxic masculinity. . .

Before another male kills himself again.
Let men be who they aspire to be
Let them enjoy things that seem "weak"
Let a man be sensitive
Let me enjoy theater over sports
Let him enjoy a "girly" drink at the bar
Let us respect our significant other

It's in our hands. . .

It is not just the action, but the buildup of it.
  The final moment when your heart
  just cannot stand the pain and suffering
All the hate for ourselves and others.
The burden of social status on our hearts.
  Yet, there is no selfless thought with this
  type of action we follow through with.
We never think of the pain we bestow upon those we love most.
Because of our mental exhaustion.
Lack of adaptation to society's manipulation.
  Out of fear of sticking and trusting that
  life will get better if we choose to do so.
So we escape the only way we think we know is best.
We take the gun, the knife, the pills, the belt, the car.
  We pull the trigger, plunge the blade, swallow them all,
  hang from above, and crash it head on.
That's it. . . it's over. . . our loved ones can clean up the mess. . .

—Suicide

practice what you preach
not lack what you speak
it's all in the results
what you have accomplished
not saying what you'll accomplish
we keep doing the same stuff
over and over again
expecting a different result

—Hypocrisy

my time is overdue
I'm just on borrowed time at this point
so many obligations, so many deadlines
I bit off more than I can chew.

too many people counting on me
but without lending a hand
it's holding me back though
from who I am supposed to be.

it foresees dark future
when I fail and lose the people
the ones who I love the most
an unforgettable torture.

—Overused

Never needed the validation from friends
Just to fit in, I'll follow all the trends.
The only likes I need are on my screen
But when I get none, my life is not so keen.
I smile in every picture I take
Too bad nobody knew that it was all just fake
People can't see my masks
Mental health has no casque.
Forget about having the perfect relationship
Oh, and include that "authentic friendship."
We only like to take our pictures
Covering all our imperfect lives, fixtures.
I only travel the world so I can achieve clout
But Instagram isn't what makes you stand out.
Our phone gives us a skewed vision
We'll never see what's real and make our own decision.
Believe the first thing we see by the news
When all those networks make money on your loose screws.
Just want to live in a world where love prevails
We can't escape that hate, insecurity will always hail.

—*Social Media Uncertainty*

your daughter can't love boys
your son can't be sensitive
we have to worship what you worship
we can't cry or show emotion
"it's all in your head" they say
we have to follow like sheep
you run from us when times are hard
but you're here to shame us
and blame us for our faults
not look on your own. . .
you're a fraud
and a deadbeat
don't forget toxic
so let me leave
let me live elsewhere
with someone who cares
someone who listens

—Bad Parenting

. . . I Want To Kiss You
. . . I Want To Touch You
. . . I Want To Make Love To You

that's all I want though

. . . I Only Want That Body
. . . I Only Want That Physique
. . . I Only Want That External

That's all I want

. . . I Don't Want Your Love
. . . I Don't Want Your Feelings
. . . I Don't Want Your Emotions

that's all I don't want

. . . So Let's Just Do This Once
. . . So Let's Just Forget It Happened
. . . So Let's Just Hookup

that's all I need

—*Objectifying*

We point the fingers but never offer solutions to the problem
No woman is asking for it
But not all men are "into it either"
Being drunk is not an excuse, but why did our friends abandon us?
They trusted you to protect them from the person at the bar. . .
But you left them
Only thinking about getting lucky instead of both being too drunk
Both consent, but it wasn't consensual
Body was lifeless, mind was empty
Life will never be the same
For both of them
Not another person can touch them and make them feel the same.
You defiled them and broke their trust with intimacy, with anyone.
This action follows no gender, no race, no political belief.
This only stems from evil, rage, violence, and selfishness.

The inner workings of demons.

—Rape

you play the victim, but in reality you're the perb. . .

i did nothing to you
but you did everything to me. . .

we do it to the environment
our minds. . .
our hearts. . .
it can come from our fossil fuels
it can come from the words we speak

    —Pollution

I am not the problem here, you are.
I do not need the world, it needs me.
The drugs are not the issue, you are the issue.
I don't have a drinking problem, more like you have a problem with me drinking.

—*Denial*

You can hold them, but no one cares
Consumes almost every aspect of your life
I let that pain go though
You should do it too
For your own sake
Not my sake
Our sake
Us

—*Grudges*

forgive yourself, because it is all you've got sometimes . . .

Leaving the bruises for everyone to see
Black eyes and blue thighs
From all the tears that were shed
Heart cold with no bold
No courage to stick up for myself
It hurts and in spurts
I cannot feel my body anymore

—Assault

I will embrace the hate
and let nobody tear me down
I will bring myself up
just to prove everyone wrong

good for nothing
just killing the lives of the innocent
all of the tax money that should not be spent

such a waste. . .

all to conquer some land
land that is not even ours to rightfully acquire
only for the oil and conquest to fill the government's lust to inspire

it will never end. . .

unless a stand we take
let your voice be heard, you yearn
to those whom it may concern

stop the fight. . .

   —*War Without Reason*

make me a martyr
so everyone else can be happy
and
be free

PART III

Balance

Wherever you are, that is where you are meant to be. . .
Nothing more and nothing less
It is keeping that equilibrium
Not to be complacent
Not to be anxious
Just be yourself
Be content but be mindful

the Yin to my Yang
the calm to my storm
the etiquette to my slang
the weird to my norm

it doesn't have to be a girl or guy
it doesn't have to be material
it doesn't have to be where you lye
it doesn't have to be trivial

where the rubber meets the road
where the good meets the evil
where the threshold meets the load
where the lost meets the retrieval

—*Stability*

the Golden Rule owns all
treat others as you would like to be treated
it is the right thing to do
even when you do not benefit from it
someone else will

I see through the smoke and mirrors
It isn't a reflection
It's objection
It keeps bringing me to tears

I have to have others bring me up
Because I can't bring up myself
I have no self-wealth
I am never enough

Do everything I can to not get stuck in oblivion
Surround myself with good people who have drive
That just want to see me thrive
Not just treat me like I am one in a billion

The thing I need is the thing you give
So make that stuff positive
And avoid the toxic negative
This is what I need in order to live

—*Energy*

Get a little, but it can go a long way
Makes the closest allies turn to enemies
Give it to the wrong person, chaos ensues
Leads to our corruption where lives are lost
Not one person can have it all
Not even ourselves. . .
We will lose our moral compass
Ethics tend to diminish
If money is this, then it's measured by millions
We should share ourselves to others then
It's the only way
It's our way

—Power

I generate it, but don't rely on it
create it like an artist
where my future is my canvas
wish me it, but don't let me use it

—*Luck*

starts off the worst but ends the best
it's the truth that needs to be heard
except it doesn't come off your chest
it comes from the actions or punishments
not so much as uplifting
more so giving your soul nourishment
it's not what we want, but what we require
take these bumps in the road
and use them to inspire
take a heartbreak for motivation
failure sometimes is a blessing
becoming the option in the situation

—*Life Lessons*

It's about what you make of it.
Isn't it simple?
Not even just for power.
But for everyone?
A day wasted is a day without production.
What about mundane tasks?
It doesn't need suits and ties.
What about money?
It's not everything, it's just an aspect.
How?
You have to have some enjoyment too.
What if I'm in a bad place?
Then leave it. . .
What if I can't?
Don't force it, to be what society says it should be. . .

      —*Work*

I never put love first, always last.
Saw it as a bad trait, but I see success.
The time and attention is toward my goals.
You're either with me or against me.
It's not selfish, it's just my livelihood.
I would rather be broke and doing what I love than rich and miserable.
I won't settle for the average, that's not me.
I will strive for perfection and excellence with all facets in life.
Not just work, but socially too.
I want friends who support my dreamer lifestyle.
A lover who helps me through the ups and downs.
I'm not selfish, I just want to be the best

—*Priorities*

I feel like I have to glow
watch out for me. . .
look a certain way
who I'm expected to be. . .
supposed to be this huge success
I work hard on the nightly
trying to make the writing perfect
changing my words ever so slightly. . .
walking the red carpet one day
make momma so proud. . .
handling life's noise that comes
silence the critics that are so loud. . .

—*Pressure Makes Diamonds*

I'll move on the way I want to move on
that might be healthy
but I might do it in an unhealthy manner too
blocking you on social media eased my mind
not responding to you comforted my soul

just leave me alone, you ended things WITH ME
you broke up WITH ME
so stop playing mind games WITH ME
you cut the ties WITH ME

It's more than just old tweets and words.
But the actions and the intentions
That defines a person
When we critique those around us,
Let's not forget our faults or fears
Or the backgrounds of our peers
Since we all live under the same roof
That roof is planet Earth
So please, show some damn respect
And not get upset over old tweets
Instead, we educate and not dictate
And unite us as one.

—*Sensitivity*

it can be healthy
also unhealthy too
it can attract
also retract too
it can progress
also regress too
it can strengthen
also weaken as well
it can unite
and segregate too
take these in baby steps
not forced with strides

—Disagreement

I wish life was like my dreams
where everybody was happy
everybody was healthy
nobody killed one another
nobody tormented each other
life is good
life is peaceful

we try to promote the positive, but sound negative
allowing too many opinions to allow us to be great
to be fit
to be active
society tells us to look a certain way
but what about our own wants?
wellness mentally and physically should be promoted
not a six pack
not an obese frame
just a look that is happy
a look that is healthy

    —Body Image

We only care what they want when it pertains to us
When in reality the past shaped them
It hurt them more than you know
You want the real feeling
While they want nothing plutonic
They just want an intimate physique to please them
We don't talk about it like we should have
So I got mad when you broke me
And I took that energy to someone else
I hurt them
Then they took the energy to hurt someone else
You see?
It is just a cycle of pain
Because we did not make things clear
We relied on "playing it by ear"
Instead of inserting boundaries
We just inserted ourselves
Where one puts their heart into it
The other is afraid to commit
Leaving a scar on your heart
Why didn't we make it clear from the start?

—Intentions

if nice guys finish where they start

then I need to change it up, so I do not finish last

don't tell me you love me
just to leave me in 8 weeks
don't bring up my confidence
just to destroy it in the end
don't tell me "it's not you it's me"
when you talk bad about me to your friends and family while sub tweeting
toxic posts thinking it will get under my skin

What kind of music do you listen to?
Is it good music that will make you feel good?
Is it music that makes you want to hurt people?
Do you feel empowered by the music?
Do you feel hatred toward a group of people?

What kind of TV do you watch?
Are they movies or shows that promote healthy habits?
Does the show or movie have an underlying message?
Is it just mindless drama?
Is it just a show to pass the time?

What is your news source?
Are they known to tell the truth?
Are they known to lie?
Are they telling you what you want to hear?
Or is news that you need to hear?

—Influences Around You

Embrace her emotions
Embrace her love
Embrace her anger
Embrace her sadness
Embrace her everything

Because one day you might lose that.

Losing that to someone else
Who doesn't micromanage
Who doesn't condescend
Who doesn't hate on her dreams
Who doesn't make her feel stuck

the street goes two ways
it is not just about your pain
and not only about your gain
this is not one of those limited stays

don't tell me you love me to reassure
if you are just going to leave
you don't leave me enough to stop my grieve
I need someone where with adversity they endure

the views do not have to be black or white
no reasons to be just elephants or donkeys
comparing straight arrows to junkies
just healthy debate or equality despite. . .

who taught you that growing up
especially with some "role models" that are living
and telling their kids to be never be giving
treating other people like garbage pickup

Burning bridges is great until you burn the bridge that takes you to the next destination. . .

Life was meant to be a mountain
Our personal Mount Everest
Something we must conquer ourselves with the help of our family and our
friends.
Just make the most of our struggles
To make them our victory stories that we can tell our own kids one day for
their inspiration
One day we will look back on life to understand that we had the obstacles
in front of us for a reason
From death to disease
Success to failure
From pride to insecurity
Temptations and influences
Virtues and Vices
The good and the evil

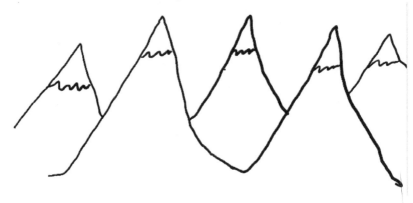

I did all that I could for everyone that I loved so dearly in my life. Whether it was for my family, my friends, my relationships, and even myself. It feels like I am never enough and never will be enough. That is until someone picks me up. What makes life so beautiful is the people that you tend to surround yourself with on a daily basis. We can either surround ourselves with people who promote us or who demote us. Those are our strongholds, so be wise about it. Pick the people who want your success just as bad as you do. With a healthy balance of life's enjoyment as well.

Speaking of fulfillment, what about that? What about our jobs? Our salaries? Our happiness with work? People tend to get caught up with money and how it makes one's problems suddenly disappear. Well, that is true but also false. Money does eliminate problems, but that is just financially. People will only love you for your money and success sometimes. They want to ride your coattails. When choosing the right job, choose something YOU want to do. Make yourself happy each day, no matter the paycheck.

A message to Millennials and Generation Z, we start at the bottom for a reason. We are not the best in our field and we sure as heck are not the brightest. This instant gratification mindset needs to stop. We must embrace the grind and our strive for perfection in a different manner. We should have the curiosity and drive for knowledge. We should crave learning; we should love the self-improvement. Then we teach others and pay it forward. That seems sensible enough. Laziness and complacency will lead to demise of everyone, no matter how rich or how powerful you can become over time. Karma is what it is.

Also, stop treating each other like they do not matter. Let's love each other, okay? Fair enough? I know we might have poor leadership and poor media management. However, it cost $0.00 to be a good person. That is not too much to ask out of everyone. I know we all have been used, abused, or objectified no matter the background. We all have been hurt by people and by events in life. That is no excuse to break other people's hearts though. Let's cut that toxicity out, seriously. Be good to one another, because we got one life to live (at least that I know of thus far). Stop attacking one another too. Stop attacking race, religion, sexual orientation, gender, or even political beliefs. This is absurd on all levels. We can be better as a human race.

The happiness. . . where is it located? How can I obtain it fully? The happiness is inside of you. It never left you. You just suppressed it with drugs, alcohol, sex, and just plain misery. We can make others happy. We can make ourselves happy. I know sometimes our brains have a chemical imbalance, but we can seek that help. We have those resources. We just need provide and promote them better. Find a venting source and find that inner peace within ourselves. That is the key to victory. That is the key to a happy life. We just need to open our minds more.

Let's build ourselves up and stop tearing others down for our simple pleasure. We are a microcosm of all things good and evil. Our lives are stories of adversity, triumph, failure, success, temptations, mediations, and everything in between. The goal should to be the best version of ourselves. Let's make the world smile.